Magic piano book

for 4 year olds

Primer Level B

For the young beginner

Lucia Timková

Teachers and Parents

This method provides solid training for beginners, from the youngest to the oldest, using easy ways to make quick progress without difficulties in understanding. To help with the teaching process, many coloured pictures and graphics use the student's visual memory to get a strong and secure grasp of the basics uses.

● Students gain an understanding of the basic important theory using many coloured pictures to prompt their visual memory to help them understand and use it in their exercises in practice songs and to practice/test it in the workbook.

● Note-reading skills. The students are to say the names of the notes aloud and count them while they play the exercises on the piano. This makes
students realize what notes they are playing, which is not easy. They don't learn it by memorising using the finger guide or by memorising the melody. Rather, they have to know the exact note names. They read notes from the very start.

● Each finger or a new note is individually and strongly developed using a lot of exercises for particular subjects from the beginning with a graduated, consistent method.

● Another strength is the introduction of ensemble playing from the very beginning. Beginner students have to play each exercise three times: say letter names while they play, count while they play, and play with a teacher. This is important for the teacher to help guide the student and to make sure that students understand the individual notes and already know how to play each exercise before they go home. When the students can read music, performing becomes a joy rather than a dreaded experience.

● In the workbook, which is included for each level you are going to confirm the notes and the theory/terminology you have learned during the lesson in three steps, which should be done in each lesson. Writing the notes, finding the notes on the staff/stave in different orders and playing the game "Noughts and Crosses" where students are drawing and explaining the symbols to help them remember it.

● After students have completed books A/B for four year olds, 1A/1B and 2A/2B, they are competent in music terminology and sight reading. They have a solid enough understanding to begin studying books of other composers; Classical or Christmas books at that particular level.

Magic Piano book 1A begins by reviewing the same concepts taught in Magic Piano A/B for four year olds and also introduces new concepts for the left hand, with progression to book 1B.

CONTENTS

This book belongs to:

_____

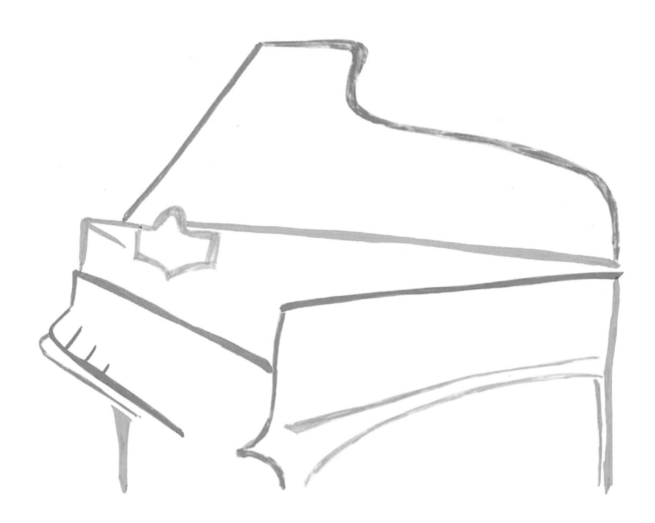

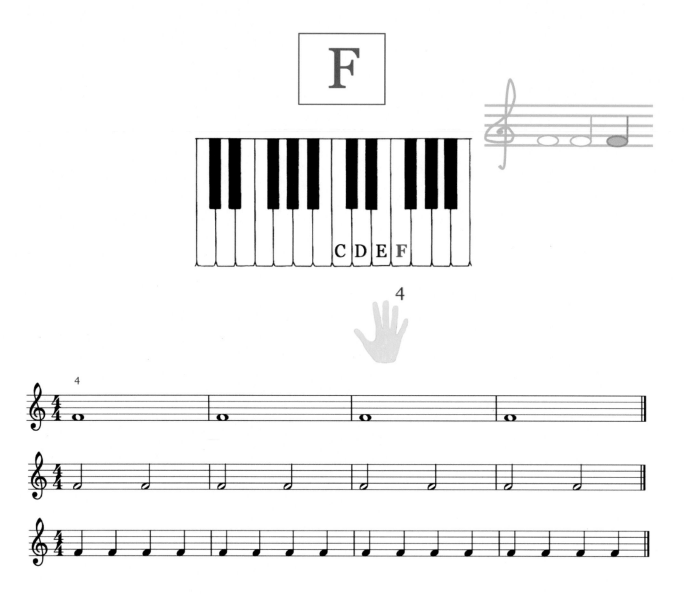

1) Play and say the letter names of the notes.
2) Play and count till four.
3) Play and listen to the song.

Frogs

1) Play and say the letter names of the notes.

2) Play and count till two.

3) Play with your teacher and listen to the song.

Accompaniment

Practising

When you prac-tice eve-ry day then it's ea-sy all to play. When you prac-tice

eve-ry day then you all know how to play.

1) Play and say the letter names of the notes.
2) Play and count till four.
3) Play with your teacher and listen to the song.

Accompaniment

Stars

Repeat sign

Repeat sign means play the piece again.

Stars are shin - ing in the sky in the eve - ning in the night.
Stars are shin - ing in the sky you can see them when it's night.

1) Play and say the letter names of the notes.
2) Play and count till four.
3) Play with your teacher and sing the song.

Accompaniment

Flowers

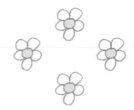

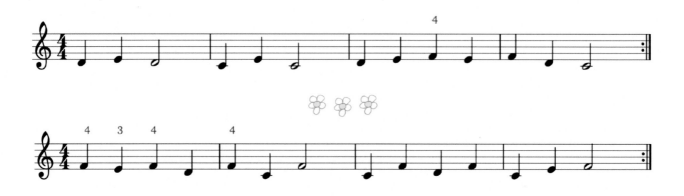

1) Play and say the letter names of the notes.

2) Play and count till four.

3) Play with your teacher and listen to the song.

Accompaniment

Accompaniment

Sunny days

Rai - ny days   win - dy days   I love on - ly   sun - ny days.

1) Play and say the letter names of the notes.
2) Play and count till four.
3) Play with your teacher and sing the song.

Accompaniment

Incomplete bar/measure

Tunes can start on any beat of the bar.
This one starts on the 4th beat.

1) Play and say the letter names of the notes.
2) Play and count till four.
3) Play and listen to the song.

Week

On Mon - day Tues - day Wednes - day Thurs - day Fri - day we go to school.

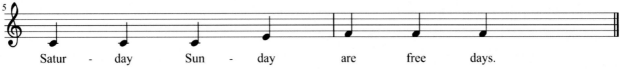

Satur - day Sun - day are free days.

1) Play and say the letter names of the notes.
2) Play and count till four.
3) Play with your teacher and sing the song.

Accompaniment

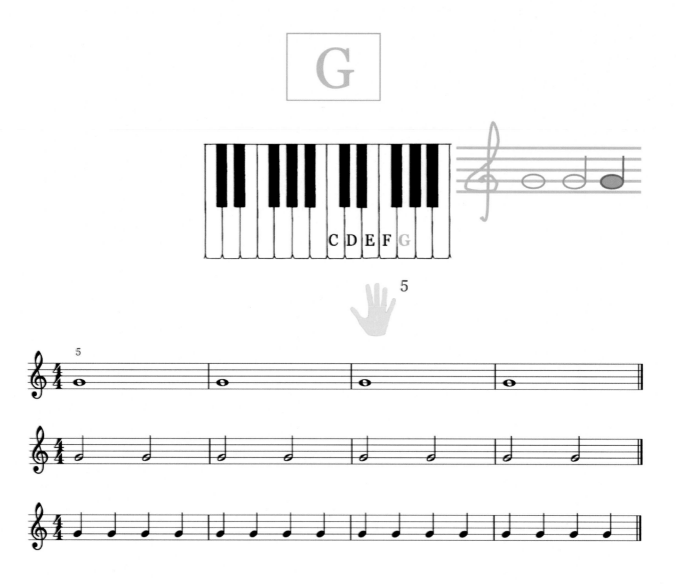

1) Play and say the letter names of the notes.

2) Play and count till four.

3) Play and listen to the song.

Holiday

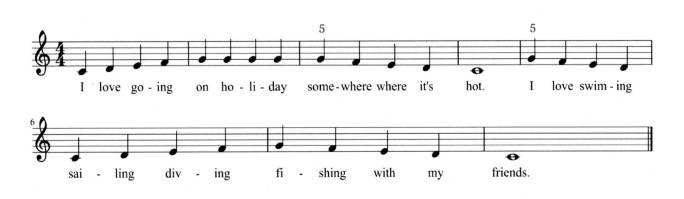

I love go - ing   on ho - li - day   some - where where it's   hot.   I   love swim - ing

sai - ling   div - ing   fi - shing   with   my   friends.

1) Play and say the letter names of the notes.

2) Play and count till four.

3) Play with your teacher and sing the song.

Accompaniment

Tidy up

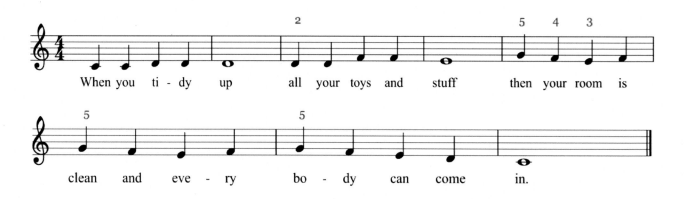

When you ti - dy up all your toys and stuff then your room is

clean and eve - ry bo - dy can come in.

1) Play and say the letter names of the notes.
2) Play and count till four.
3) Play with your teacher and sing the song.

Accompaniment

Mary had a little lamb

Traditional

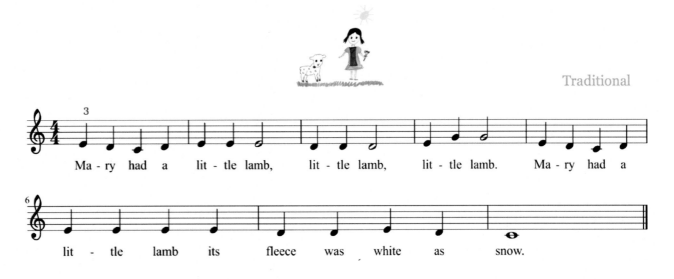

Ma - ry had a lit - tle lamb, lit - tle lamb, lit - tle lamb. Ma - ry had a

lit - tle lamb its fleece was white as snow.

1) Play and say the letter names of the notes.
2) Play and count till four.
3) Play with your teacher and sing the song.

Accompaniment - Student plays one octave higher

Little Bo-Peep

Traditional

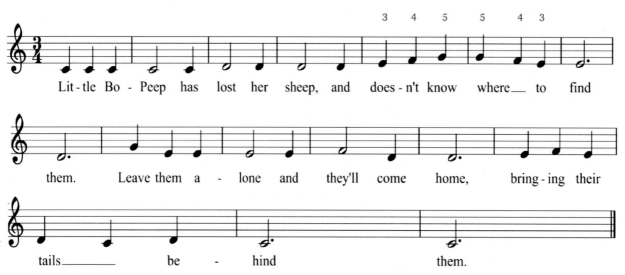

Lit-tle Bo - Peep has lost her sheep, and does-n't know where__ to find

them. Leave them a - lone and they'll come home, bring-ing their

tails_____ be - hind them.

1) Play and say the letter names of the notes.
2) Play and count till free,
3) Play with your teacher and sing the song.

Accompaniment

14

Eensy Weensy Spider

Traditional

Een - sy ween - sy spi - der went up the wa - ter spout. Down came the rain and

washed the spi - der out. Out came the sun and dried up all the rain and the

een - sy ween - sy spi - der went up the spout a - gain!

1) Play and say the letter names of the notes.
2) Play and count till four.
3) Play with your teacher and sing the song.

Accompaniment

Twinkle, Twinkle, Little Star

Accompaniment

Twinkle, Twinkle, Little Star

Traditional

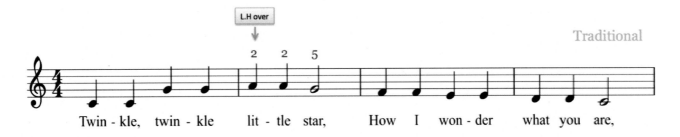

Twin - kle, twin - kle   lit - tle   star,   How   I   won - der   what   you   are,

Up   a - bove   the   world   so   high,   Like   a   dia - mond   in   the   sky.

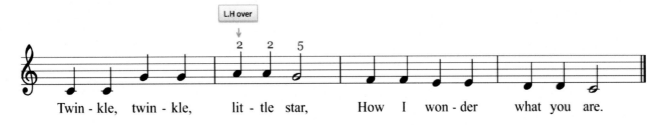

Twin - kle,   twin - kle,   lit - tle   star,   How   I   won - der   what   you   are.

1) Play and say the letter names of the notes.
2) Play and count till four.
3) Play with your teacher and sing the song.

17

Jingle Bells

Traditional

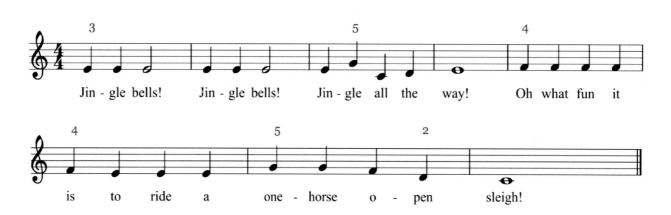

Jin - gle bells!   Jin - gle bells!   Jin - gle all the way!   Oh what fun it

is   to   ride   a   one - horse   o - pen   sleigh!

1) Play and say the letter names of the notes.

2) Play and count till four.

3) Play with your teacher and sing the song.

Accompaniment

Ode to Joy

L.van Beethoven

1) Play and say the letter names of the notes.
2) Play and count till four.
3) Play with your teacher.

Accompaniment

Certificate

This is to certify that

_____

successfully completed

Magic piano book B

on

_____

and is eligible for promotion to

Magic piano book 1A

Congratulations!

_____

Teacher's signature

This course is carefully leveled into the following books :

Magic piano book for 4 year olds - Primer Level A   ISBN-13: 978-1490375946

Magic piano book for 4 year olds - Primer Level B   ISBN-13: 978-1490997391

Magic work book for 4 year olds - Primer Level A-B   ISBN-13: 978-1490997780

Magic piano book - Level 1A - For Beginners   ISBN-13: 978-1499722758

Magic piano book - Level 1B - For Beginners   ISBN-13: 978-1499723243

Magic work book - Level 1A-1B - For Beginners   ISBN-13: 978-1499723816

Magic piano book - Level 2A   ISBN-13: 978-1490999050

Magic piano book - Level 2B   ISBN-13: 978-1490999111

Magic work book - Level 2A-2B   ISBN-13: 978-1490999159

Sinterklaasliedjes – Niveau 2   ISBN-13: 978-1499724202

Made in the USA
San Bernardino, CA
29 June 2017